MW01095053

Thinking Inside
the Crease

Thinking Inside the Crease

THE MENTAL SECRETS TO BECOMING A DOMINANT LACROSSE GOALIE

Christian K Buck

Copyright © 2016 Christian K Buck
All rights reserved.
ISBN: 1519125984
ISBN-13: 9781519125989
Library of Congress Control Number: 2016903143
CreateSpace Independent Publishing Platform
North Charleston, South Carolina

Dedication

This book is dedicated to all the lacrosse goalies of the world, from amateur to professional, who are passionate about playing the position and are driven to being the very best they can be.

Table of Contents

Acknowledgments

First and foremost, I want to thank my wife, Gail, for all her love and support. I couldn't do it without her. I am extremely grateful to everyone who has helped me become who I am today: My parents, George and Dianne; my mentor, Dave; Coaches Alex, Skip, Keith, Kip, John, and Adam. Lastly, I want to acknowledge all the goalies who have given me the privilege of working with them over the last twenty years.

Introduction

I'm a goalie...at least I was one at one time. Today, I coach lacrosse goalies of all levels all over the United States and Canada on a critical component of playing the position that's completely neglected: the mental game. So many psychological factors effect goalies, yet goalies often simply rely on what comes naturally to them (for better or worse) when instead they could be using learned skills and tools to navigate the game successfully.

Some of these psychological aspects are: Lowering internal and external interference; Dealing with anxiety; Recognizing and addressing the physiological effects of fear; Conditioning thought processes to consistently focus on the next shot and disregard the previous one; Pre-game preparation and routines; Optical optimization (using the rods and cones of the eyes to increase our chances of finding the release point of the shot); Playing to win instead of trying to perform or impress; Dealing with being the back-up; and How to get on the field as the starter.

After working with goalies for over 10 years as a mental coach and goalie psychology specialist, I have many clients who have embraced these concepts and found success on the college level at schools such as Loyola, UVA, Hopkins, Drexel, Ohio State, Notre Dame, Syracuse, Georgetown, Rutgers, Tufts, Amherst, Union, etc., as well as professionally in the MLL. The success of these goalies is due, in part, to their great technique, but more importantly, to their relentless commitment to work every day at improving their mental game, every practice - in season or out. It is my belief that playing sports is 100% physical and 100% mental.

Let me give you a personal example. When I was playing in college, I finally got the starting spot at the end of my freshman year. In the Fall of my sophomore year, a transfer-student came to our program who was a pretty good goalie. Even though I was the starter the previous Spring, he was named the starter on the first day of fallball.

I spent the next six months determined to get the starting job back. I worked out in the gym every day after practice. I lapped the team during sprints (which the rest of the team was not too happy about - but

I was determined to show the coaches that I meant business). I listened to heavy music to get myself fired up and mentally prepared for every practice. Each day was like "Game Day" for me. High Intensity. Focused. Go Hard. Every day.

And it worked. By the start of the season, I was named the starting goalie once again.

I played well in the first game even though we lost a close one to a pretty good team. I got the game ball for our win in the second game. I was feeling good... but I also started feeling the pressure that I had to keep playing well if I wanted to keep the starting spot. I knew I was on a very short leash with no room for mistakes.

In the third game, playing against our biggest rival, the pressure mounted. I knew I had to play well again and as each shot went by me, I could feel myself getting more and more tense. I couldn't save a beach ball that day. I let in 14. The most I had ever let in in my entire career was 9. Heck, I only lost one game in four years of high school.

But 14 goals against us was enough for me to get the hook. I didn't start the next game. In fact, I never played in a game again. Looking back, I now realize **I was so busy trying to keep my job, I didn't do my job.**

In that expression is the key to success in the cage. Our job as goalies is not to perform well, impress coaches, or keep the starting job. Our job is to stop the ball. Period. End of story.

Think about the best game you ever played. I would imagine there was minimal psychological interference when you were making saves in that game. The ball seemed like it was in slow-motion. Am I right? You can still visualize what it was like on that day when everything came easily. This book was written to help you 1.) Figure out why you played the way you did that day, and 2.) Learn to play like that more consistently, because playing consistently is purely mental.

This book is written for goalies so they don't make the same mistakes I did. Had I known during my college career what I know now, that might not have been my last game as a starter. Although, that last game was probably the reason I ultimately went on to earn my Masters Degree in sport psychology and find a career I love as a mental/performance coach and sport psychology consultant. By imparting this knowledge on to you, my hope is you can avoid a similar experience, simply because you have the wrong mindset.

I felt the need to write this book because, in my experience, I recognize lacrosse goalies don't get the attention they need or deserve; nor are goalies (or coaches) focusing on all the components that will allow goalies to play their best in the cage. I hope after reading this book that will change.

Hopefully after learning the mental skills necessary to enhance your play, you will play at a level you never thought possible. Playing with confidence, passion, and a little bit of swagger.

Think like an All-American first, then become one, not the other way around...

CHAPTER 1

Talent – Interference +/- Luck

You listen to the coach talk about last minute preparations about how to handle their offense. "#45 has a lefty rip. Remember that," you say to yourself before the championship. As you warm up, you focus on the release point, watching exactly where the ball comes out of the coach's stick. You start to check your anxiety levels: Are you too amped up or perfectly balanced with a relaxed aggression? You make sure you are yelling loudly and aggressively in pre-game 6 v 6.

"Okay, I am fired up. I'm ready. I have prepared for this moment my whole life. This is my time. Let's go. Get it done!"

If you want to play your best in the cage, you must be prepared. As preparation increases, so does confidence. And as confidence increases, anxiety decreases. So how do we accomplish this?

First, let's take a look at the components of performance. Dr. Rick Jensen, a world-renowned sport psychologist, breaks down performance into three categories: Talent, Interference, and Luck. His equation shows us a way to digest how these components interact with one another and allow us to prepare more appropriately:

Performance = Talent – Interference +/- Luck

Talent

Talent can be defined as the sum of a goalie's physical, strategic, and technical skills. Although a player's performance on any given day cannot ultimately be controlled, his level of talent going into a game can be. Fortunately, talent is controlled by the quality of your training. Your training program may include a range of multidisciplinary areas, including instruction, practice, fitness, active rest, nutrition, etc. These areas combine to form a player's talent. I think of it as the "physical" part of the equation.

To improve talent, you must work on weaknesses, like improving your foot speed by jumping rope or implementing that new arc you were taught during practice so that it will become second-nature for game day.

Improving your talent does not happen magically. Quite simply, hard work and effort improve talent. You must put in the hours in the cage, on the track, and in the weight room.

Whether you play in college or just starting to learn the position, there are always ways to improve your talent. During "individuals" in college, or practice in youth league, make sure you have a coach help you with your technique.

The most important part of your technique in the cage is your angles. Your "angles" describe how square you are to the shooter. Make sure that your stick, shoulders, hips, and feet are always perpendicular to the shooter. If your angles are off, every save will be that much more difficult to make. On the other hand, if your angles are good, you give yourself the best chance at stopping the ball.

Another issue poor angles present is, combined with fear, they can have a devastating affect on your stance, but we will discuss this more in Chapter 2. If your angles are off to begin with, and then you physiologically respond poorly before the shot, you will find it extremely difficult to move smoothly and assertively through the save.

A goalie's "talent" also includes both the ability to clear the ball and stick skills. If you want to be the best goalie you can be, you must improve in all aspects of the position. Be sure to play wallball and work both the strong- and off-hand. Yes, your OFF-hand! You will need it every once in a while, so be sure you can pass consistently. Also, make sure you understand the general principles of clearing. Find the 2 on 1. Be able to get up field if need be. Learn different outlet passes. All of this adds to your level of talent.

Interference

Interference is the mental part of this equation and can be defined as anything that detracts from your talent. There are countless distractions that work against the goalie's ability to make saves.

Interference can be internal or external. You can experience external interference from the weather, the other team, your team, the venue, field conditions, fans, parents, the new pocket you're not sure about yet, etc. Additionally, interference can come from internal sources, such as fatigue, emotional disturbance, anxiety, and fear. According to the Talent–Interference+/-Luck formula, you will benefit the most when your interference score is "zero." If you keep your interference near zero, you give yourself the best chance of performing at your highest level, allowing your talent to show through.

The time to learn how to manage internal and external interference is now, during practice, before you find yourself in the State Championship unprepared. You can't wait until the game to implement new thought processes or strategies. You must cultivate the right mental strategies so that they are ingrained in your thinking process, becoming second nature. Just like improving your talent, you must WORK on your mental game.

Start reducing your interference during practice in order for your talent to shine. The best way to stop the ball is to be completely focused on the release and contact point with an aggressive mindset. That's it. No distractions, which is not easy. Learn to focus on the appropriate cues to make stops in practice, every day, so when game-time comes, you are ready.

When it's game-time, interference, unlike talent, must be monitored and managed. You must take the time to identify the sources of interference that most effect your game, then design and implement coping strategies to deal with them.

For example, one way to deal with the anxiety of a game is to embrace your nerves. Sports are meant to raise the heart rate. People suffering from anxiety disorders experience the same symptoms as the ten players stepping on the court to start the Final Four. But who would trade positions with anyone on that stage? Embrace the excitement and competitive anxiety of tournaments. It's why you play sports in the first place!

Interference is very difficult to control if left unattended but you can learn how to control with mental skills training. Reduce your interference and let your talent shine.

Luck

Luck is defined as the fluctuations in performance due to chance. The most common displays of luck for a goalie are when the ball hits someone's stick and deflects into the goal, or you make the save but someone grabs the rebound and easily dunks it in because you were out of position. This could be considered bad luck, or good luck, depending on which team you are on. Over time, luck should follow statistical laws of averages, so you will have your fair share of both.

When something bad happens merely by chance during a game or scrimmage, recognize that luck DOES play a part in the game. Accept it, and move on. Dwelling on bad luck only adds to interference. There is no psychological benefit to rethinking and reevaluating an act of bad luck.

Performance = Talent – Interference +/- Luck

Focus on increasing your talent. No matter your current playing level, you can always improve your talent. Learn how to limit (or eliminate) the interference you experience before or during games by working on it in practice. (Find the release point. Find the contact point. Play with an aggressive mindset.) Recognize and accept what is luck. If you do these things, no matter what happens in the game that day, you'll know you have prepared the best you could. Nobody can ask for more.

In this book, we will be focusing on the Interference component of the formula. While improving your talent is a imperative for success, Fear, Anxiety, Confidence and Mental Toughness are all key elements for you to overcome or master in order to reduce internal interference and become the best goalie you can be.

Recap:

- The key to improving performance is to increase your talent (physical) and decrease your interference (mental).
- Be sure to focus on improving your talent on a daily basis.
- Talent can increase and decrease only incrementally. Interference can fluctuate wildly.
- By intensely focusing on release and contact points, you will reduce interference.
- Responding to bad luck poorly will contribute to internal interference.

CHAPTER 2

Fear

You're man-down. The ball moves from your right side across the crease to an attackman who is alone on the left. He catches it and reaches back for a ten-yard blast. As he is setting his feet to rip upper corner, what are you thinking? How will you respond?

As goalies, we hope that our reactions are instinctual, but unfortunately, that's not always the case. Sometimes fear takes over. You may flinch, close your eyes, or drop to your knees. Fear can affect you to a point where you may not be able to control your muscles and you actually feel paralyzed. But where does the fear come from?

After playing the position and working with goalies for over 30 years now (including my time spent as mental coach and goalie psychology specialist),

I have come to learn the most important aspect of playing in the cage:

THE PHYSIOLOGICAL EFFECTS OF FEAR ARE THE SINGLE MOST DEBILITATING FACTOR OF PLAYING GOALIE IN LACROSSE.

You can focus on improving your technique all day long, but it will do you no good if you don't address the fear you experience when someone is about to wind up and shoot on you. You must address how fear affects your play in order to reduce interference and show your true talent. Period. (And, by the way, everyone experiences some sort of fear while playing in the cage; it's just to what degree that makes the difference.)

Goalies can experience fear for a variety of reasons in the cage. Probably the most common fear when playing goalie is the fear of pain. This makes sense. Getting hit hurts. Plain and simple. We all remember that one shot we took in the leg, bicep, or shoulder that didn't stop stinging for days, not to mention the bruise that followed for much longer than that.

A second reason we may experience fear is the inherent desire to not let down our teammates. It is our responsibility as goalies to stop the ball, even if the defense collapses. It could be that you are simply afraid to fail. That's what makes you an athlete. Nicholls (1984, 1989) states in his Achievement Motivation Theory that an athlete's major motive is to demonstrate competence. Fear can take over your ability to make stops if that competence is threatened.

Notice I did not list a last second shot at the end of a close game as an example of a situation where we experience fear. In that situation, a goalie may experience high levels of *anxiety*, not fear. What's the difference? I'll tell you.

Anxiety and fear are closely related negative emotional states associated with physical or psychological harm. These emotions can be differentiated by the relationship between the feeling and the potential threat.

Anxiety is characterized by the anticipation of being harmed in the *future*. Fear is characterized as the anticipation of being harmed in the *present*. For example, a high state of anxiety can occur when we worry about an upcoming test, asking that girl to prom, or how well you will do in tryouts. In these situations, the feeling of anxiousness is vague and is not presently "dangerous."

Fear, on the other hand, is a reaction to *immediate* danger. This distinction is important to recognize because, unlike anxiety, fear can have highly debilitating effects when trying to make a stop in goal. Let me explain.

In the scenario discussed earlier, the goalie is anticipating a fast, hard shot from someone who is wide open at a relatively close range. At this point, a part of the brain, called the Limbic System and particularly the Amygdala, springs into action. This part of the brain is the emotional center and is responsible for protecting the body from harm. For instance, it is the mechanism that causes you to flinch if a door slams behind you or causes you to recoil if someone were to point a gun at you. (Let's hope that never happens, but you get my point...)

Once the limbic system is activated, it sets off a chain of events that will inhibit you from performing easily and fluidly, thus making it incredibly difficult to make the stop.

First, the body fills with chemicals called Norepinephrine and Adrenaline. With this rush of chemicals, the heart rate increases and the muscles tighten.

As the muscles tighten, you may find yourself "shrinking" in the cage. Have you ever dropped to your knees to make a save before they even shot the ball? That "collapsing" reaction is the brain's way of protecting the body from immediate harm. Your brain says, "Get out of the way! This is going to hurt!" The same is true for closing your eyes, ducking your head, or tucking in your elbows to your sides.

Fear effects us during the shot, so now what? First of all, it's paramount you become aware of these thoughts and reactions because without acknowledging your thoughts, you cannot change them. Once acknowledged, there are two ways to address the fear.

First, become aware of your tendencies when someone is winding up. Watching film is critical to learning your tendencies, but don't just the watch the saves. You have to watch the goals you let in too. Observing how you react during those goals is much more valuable than simply watching the saves you made.

When you watch the shots you let in, can you see your body tighten? Do you lower you hands? Is it difficult to move your feet quickly because you are in a squat position? Can you move your hands as quickly as you would like? Do your eyes flinch? Do you tuck you chin down and lower your head? Do you drop one or both knees towards the ground?

Once you've established your debilitating tendencies, you have the power to counteract the part of the brain that is trying to protect you. Keep your hands loose. Drop you shoulders (but not your hands). Exaggerate your step and force yourself to move towards the ball. Keep your eyes wide open. Whatever your tendencies are, make sure you address them and adjust accordingly.

Remember, we know that physiologically our body wants to remain in one spot and "shrink" to protect itself during the shot. Knowing that is the case, you must force yourself to move forward and stay loose.

Second, you want to de-emphasize the effects of fear by focusing on the release and not the ensuing danger. You can train your mind to become so focused on the release point of the shot that the limbic system never gets activated in the first place, and you remain comfortable and ready to move. It is a technique called "Lock In, Lock Out." By locking in to the appropriate stimulus (in this case, the release point of the impending shot), we lock out the potential pain of getting hit.

You CAN change your mindset when facing shots, and if you do, fear will start to disappear. You can "get angry" at the shooter, raising your intensity level. Choose to go all out and stop the ball. Be in an aggressive mindset BEFORE the shot is even in the air.

Let me give you an example: When I was working with a lacrosse team in Arizona, we put on a clinic for the public at a Phoenix Sports Day to show the community what lacrosse was all about. About twenty high school players displayed what they do in practice from shooting, passing, defending, and so on.

Unfortunately, we did not have a high school goalie there that day, so I jumped in cage for the demonstration. The players got in line to run towards the goal and take a shot on me, one by one.

The first player ran all the way down to about three yards outside the crease and shot pretty much as hard as they could. I was not prepared for such a hard shot considering this was supposed to be just a demonstration. The shot hit me square on the thigh.

So, the next player in line comes down towards me in the goal - same as the first player. What happened? The same thing. Hits me, literally, right in the same spot. Not fun.

Now, the third player in line is ready to go. But this time I was not going to approach the shot so passively. I decided that if I was going to get hit, it was going to be on my terms, not the shooter's.

As they came down towards me, I started to move out and challenged them. As they shot the ball, I did everything I could to get in front of the ball. I threw my body at the ball and it hit me in the shoulder. It may have been a little painful, but I was excited to feel the pain this time. I *made* that stop, I wasn't simply hit by the ball. That bruise was a badge of honor.

Another example is when I was working with a goalie who was about to warm up for the State Championship. As we walked out to the goal before the game, I asked her, "Are you going to play in college?"

"No."

"So, this is possibly the last time you will play organized lacrosse?"

"I guess so."

"Well then, let's go see how many bruises you can get."

"Okay!"

(She had 16 saves and won the State Championship)

It comes down to a "Fight or Flight" mode. Either you are going to fight when confronted with fear, or you're going to flee. Choose to fight! If you fight you will make more saves, play better, and increase your confidence. You'll find if you fight, you'll actually get hit less often because you are more focused on the ball.

Recap:

- Fear is the single most debilitating factor of playing goalie in lacrosse.
- Fear is the anticipation of being harmed in the present, while anxiety is the anticipation of being harmed in the future.
- Fear before a shot will cause you to close your eyes, duck your head, tuck your elbows into your sides, and bring your knees together.
- Get into "fight mode" well before a shot is taken.
- Your desire to stop the ball must be greater than the fear of getting hit or letting up a goal.

- Lock into the release point to lock out the negative impending possibilities of the shot.
- Reframe your mind from being afraid of getting hit to trying to earn your bruises!

CHAPTER 3

One Shot at a Time

One of the most important aspects of playing goalie is to condition your mind to constantly focus on the NEXT shot. The next shot will ALWAYS be more important than the last one. No exceptions. Ever.

Let's examine this further. Let's say that you let up a goal (which will happen by the way - there aren't too many shutouts in lacrosse anymore). What will you think about? How will you react?

Many goalies tend to get upset about letting in a goal. It can start to consume them. "How could you let that in?!" they might yell at themselves. "That was such an easy save!" It can be difficult to let go of a shot you let in. But you must let it go nonetheless.

Playing goalie is difficult enough as it is with out being distracted by focusing on the past. You need to constantly be focused on the release of THE NEXT SHOT.

Thinking about what happened in the past has absolutely no value. Thinking about the goal you let in will only add to, and compound, your internal interference.

What if you let in two goals in a row? Then what? Then a third? I once worked with a college basketball player who told me that if he shot 0 for 2 from the floor to start the game, he would then have a terrible game. I asked him, "What if you went 8 for 10 from the field? Would you be happy shooting 80%?" Of course, he said he would be very happy to shoot 80%. But then I asked, "So it's just about missing the first two shots that you are worried about?" The point is, you are going to let in some shots, what order you let them in is irrelevant. It's part of the game. So if you let in a couple goals in the beginning of the game, it's okay. It happens. Let it go and focus on the next shot.

The best mindset for stopping the ball is total immersion in the shot you're about to save, and after you've saved that one, total immersion in the next one. The past is relevant only in terms of what it can teach you about the next shot, and the future does not extend beyond your intentions for the next shot ahead of you.

I hear a lot of goalies say that they need to make the first save in order to gain momentum, or "get into" a game. While I understand that philosophy, it's just that - a philosophy. I would argue that if you feel you the need to make the first save in order to get momentum, you are not prepared properly in the first place. You must perfect your pre-game routine so that you are in the right mindset from the beginning. Use your warm-up to prepare psychologically. Know before you hit the field what your plan is for the day: High intensity, focus on the release, commit to EVERY shot (including warm-ups).

If you are one of those goalies who feel you need to make the first save to "get into the game," make that 'first save' in warm-ups during 6 on 6. If your coach does not dedicate a section of your pre-game warm-up to 6 on 6, ask him if he would put it into the pre-game routine, even if just for a few minutes. It will simulate game conditions which allows you to mimic shots you will see in the game and gets the adrenaline flowing before the first whistle.

You cannot depend on playing with momentum. It is a very slippery slope to do so. If you depend on making that first save to have a good game, you sure are putting a lot of pressure on the first save, aren't you?

But let's think about it in another way: If positive momentum is what you need to enhance your play, negative momentum will have the same effect. If you let a couple in, and your play is based on momentum, now what? It is easy to fall into the "It's just not my day" mentality.

Tiger Woods, at one point maybe the world's most mentally tough athlete, had what I believed to be the greatest routine in golf especially when he had hit a bad shot. He allowed himself ten seconds to get upset. And if you ever get the chance to watch him play, you will definitely see him get upset. He yells at himself, throws his club at his golf bag, and starts to mutter to himself. But you will never see him carry that anger into the next shot. He has conditioned himself mentally to let go of a bad shot after ten seconds. So, he does allow himself to react and get upset, but then he moves on.

You could do something similar. Let yourself get upset. It's natural. After letting in a goal, I advise my goalies to toss the ball to the ref and talk to the defense about what may have gone wrong on the previous play. There may have been a missed slide, a wrinkle in your man-down defense, whatever.

When you're done with that, turn and face the goal. Let yourself be upset for a few seconds. Then turn around and face back up field. When you turn back around for the ensuing face-off, make sure you are ready to face the NEXT SHOT. The act of turning around and facing the goal then facing up field when you are ready will help you release the last goal.

In the Mental Conditioning Department of the IMG Academies in Bradenton, FL, they use a process or routine called "Release, Replan, Refocus." It goes like this: RELEASE a goal that has just been scored. It's in the past. Let it go. Like Tiger, get upset for ten seconds if you want. It's natural so don't fight your initial reaction. But, after you release the goal in that ten second span, start to adjust your focus back to the next shot ahead of you.

Then, REPLAN what you will do to prepare for the next shot: What is working for you? What did you learn from the last shot? Was the shooter a lefty or righty? If the shooter is more dominant with one hand, tell his defender which way you would like him to shadow that shooter in order to force him to shoot with his off-hand. Or do you talk to the entire defense to have them slide earlier when that shooter continues to dodge with his dominant hand? Or both? Who knows? It's up to you. It's your defense. Let them know what you are thinking. The important thing is that you start to focus on what the new plan is so that you don't have the same result on the next shot.

Finally, REFOCUS. Refocus your mind to the NEXT SHOT. By the time you go through the Release and Replan phases after you let in a goal, the face-off should be close to underway. This is the time for you to start focusing on the ball once again. Even though the ball is at midfield, train your eyes to follow the ball. It doesn't need to be an intense gaze. You are simply trying to regain focus to the present, not the past. Refocus on the ball, same as you did at the start of the game.

By working on this process, you will become much more consistent. Consistency is mental. Ingrain a mental process that works for you. This must be practiced.

The NEXT SHOT will always, always, always be more important than the last one.

Recap:

- You must condition your mind to stay in the present and constantly turn your focus to the next shot.
- The next shot is the only shot that will ever matter.
- Focusing on a shot in the past or in the future will only add to your interference.
- Create a post-goal routine that allows to you release the last shot, replan what is working for you and what is not, and then refocus on the next shot.

CHAPTER 4

Release Point / Contact Point

So now that you have learned how to address your fear and condition your brain to focus on one shot at a time, it is time to discuss what to focus on. I believe once you have built solid technique and perfected your angles, the singular most important component to playing goalie, is finding the Release Point and the Contact Point of every shot.

What is the Release Point? The release point is the exact spot on the top of the shooter's stick head where the ball leaves the shooter's stick. Whether it is overhand, underhand, 3/4, or sidearm, it is imperative that you find the ball at the point of release.

One day I put a video recorder in the goal and filmed someone taking shots from all different release points. Before I watched the film, as a goalie I would focus on the general area around the shooters helmet and shoulder, thinking that that was where the shot would be coming from. However, what I learned from the film was astonishing. The release point is at least two to three feet away from the shooter's shoulder.

Think about someone shooting sidearm on you. The shooter will extend his hand out to his side as far as he can in order to generate the most amount of speed. Then, add the length of the stick to the length of his arms. Now the release point is three or four feet from the ear on his shooting side – much farther away from his shoulder than I had originally thought.

The Contact Point, on the other hand, is the exact spot in space where you make contact with ball.

That contact could be with your stick or with any part of the body. Neurological studies show that the eyes cannot continually stay focused on a projectile traveling over a certain speed.

What happens is that our eyes will take several pictures of the object in motion - as if you were taking individual pictures with your eyes and not a continual stream. Your eyes cannot stay continuously focused on the ball itself due to the speed of the shot. So what happens is that your eyes will fast forward to where the ball will ultimately end up (the contact point).

Why is this important? In order to stop the ball moving as fast as it is, especially on the college level (114 mph, Really?), you must give yourself as much time as possible to see the ball at the Contact Point. If you don't see the ball until it is already half way to the goal, you will have very little chance of stopping it before it hits the net.

So in order to give yourself the best chance of stopping the ball, you need to see the ball in the air in its entirety. If the shot is initiated 12 yards from the goal, it makes sense that it would help to see the ball during the whole 12 yards. Find the release of every shot. It is the most important thing you can do to stop the ball - besides good angles and technique, of course.

This is where fear can be an enormous detriment. Very often, even the best goalies will dip their eyes or lower their head due to a fear response during the shot. If the ball is in the air from a time-and-room shot, fear can force you to dip your head or squint your eyes, therefore making it almost impossible to see the contact point.

Does this happen to you? Work really hard at keeping your chin up. One technique I have had goalies try is to look through the second (lower) section of their face mask in order to force themselves to keep their chin up.

Second, completely commit to finding the contact point. As I study more and more goalies in high school, college, even the MLL, it is obvious to me that the biggest detriment to their play, other than fear, is not being able to find the contact point. I've seen goalies actually watch the ball go by them, all the way into the net, but do not make the stop because they are falling backwards or their stick is parallel to the shot path as it's going by/in.

Be aggressive when committing to the contact point, keep your angles and choose to move forward. I recently worked with a goalie who is also a wrestler. He was having the same issues a lot of goalies have in which he was moving backwards from the shot - a fear response. He said that when he wrestles, he feels like it is him against the other wrestler and that he "owned" the other guy. I told him to do the same thing to the shooter. Tell yourself as he is winding up, "I own you!" This way, you will reframe how you go about stopping the shot and eventually it will become easier to see the contact point.

A drill I like to do with my goalies to emphasize finding the release and contact point is to have them take shots like any other drill, but the goalie has to finish the save outside the crease. Force yourself to keep moving through the contact point. It will prevent you from moving backwards in the same direction as the ball.

Another drill to aid in finding the release is to use four or five different colored balls. Put your head down before the shooter picks up a ball. Have him yell, "Shot!" midway through his shot as the ball is in the air. The objective is to detect the ball in the air and call out the color of the ball before you make contact with it.

Another great drill to really hone in on your ability to find the contact point is what I call, "Break the Glass." Here's how it works: As you are standing in the goal on your arc, in a ready position, imagine there is a pane of glass a foot in front of your stick that stretches ten feet high and ten feet wide. Picture yourself behind this huge pane of glass as the coach or partner shoots on you.

The object of the drill is to stop the ball before it breaks the imaginary pane of glass. If your contact point is in front of the glass, you did it correctly – theoretically leaving the pane of glass in tact. If not, the glass was broken and you probably made contact with the ball behind you, or at least deep into your stance. Have the shooter ask you after every shot, "Did you save the glass?" Answer "Yes" if you made contact with the ball in front of the glass. Answer "No" if the shot would have gone through the imaginary pane. It is very important that you ask that question each time; otherwise you are just stopping shots without any real intention. All drills must have a purpose with an intention to improve your talent.

It is imperative you find the release and contact point. Without doing it, you are just guessing.

"Hoping" you make the stop. Allowing fear to take over, forcing you to tuck your chin and close your eyes. If you can't see it, you can't stop it. You must work diligently at seeing the ball all the way from the release to where you make contact with the shot.

Recap:

- The release point is the point at which the ball comes out of the shooter's stick.
- The release point is usually much farther from the shooter's ear than you would expect (roughly 3-4 feet from the shooting shoulder).
- The contact point is the point at which is make direct contact with the ball.
- If you don't find the contact point, you are just guessing or hoping the ball hits you.
- The contact point should always be in front of you.
- Use the "Break the Glass" drill to hone your skill at finding the contact point.

CHAPTER 5

"Bring It!"

Recently, I have been working with some of the best goalies in the country on a mindset that I call "Bring It!" You can change your mindset from being intimidated and fearful to one of confidence and pure commitment to each shot.

Let's start with a question: If you were picking goalies for your fantasy lacrosse team, would you choose the goalie who is technically very sound but can be fearful or timid at times, or would you choose the goalie who is extremely aggressive and confident but doesn't have the best technique?

I have asked that question a hundred times and never has anyone answered they would choose the technically sound but timid goalie. Everyone chooses the aggressive, confident goalie with so-so technique. Why?

Because when it comes down to it, technique is not the most important factor for being a great goalie.

Let's look at golf for a minute. Arnold Palmer, Jack Nicklaus, Chi Chi Rodriguez, Gary Player, Tiger Woods, Phil Michelson, and Bobby Jones are some of the best golfers of all time. The best to have ever played the sport.

But, if you look at their swings, they are all very different. Their style or technique is not the relevant part of their success; it is whether or not they hit the ball solidly. That's it. They can strike the ball solidly in any given situation whether it be on the practice range or in a Major championship.

Goalies are the same way. Look at John Galloway, Kip Turner, Adam Ghitelman, Jesse Schwartzman, Niko Amato, Quint Kessenich, Brian Dougherty, Trevor Tierney and Scott Rogers. All of them are very different. Notice how Galloway plays compared to Rogers. They have very different styles, but both are exceptional in their own right.

So what's the point? The point is that *how* you make stops is irrelevant. What's important is that you make the stops in the first place. And what all those goalies from the past have in common is that they all had the right mindset that made them the best.

That mindset is aggressive. It's confident. It's the type of mindset that you can almost see. It makes the whole team better just to be around players like that. If we know fear is the greatest threat to moving to the ball smoothly during a save, then **your desire to stop**

the ball has to be greater than the fear of letting it in or getting hurt. It's that simple.

The "Bring it!" mindset means that you want the other team to shoot. You feel it in your bones that you will make the stop. That ball is yours! It is a mindset that is ripe for championships. If your mindset is timid, only hoping to play well, you won't. You must cultivate a mindset that is dominant. You are the best. No shooter can best the talent you have, that you have earned. C'mon! BRING IT!!!

During your warm up, start thinking, "Bring It!" on each shot. Every shot. Say this to yourself over and over - especially before games. It will give you a positive reframe to each shot, changing from a fearful response to one of attitude and swag. "Bring it! I own you!" This mindset is much more powerful, and you will notice how much more aggressively you will play. By applying this exercise before games, it will put you in an incredibly powerful state of mind that will continue into the game. (You can also do this at halftime to refresh.)

Another way to automatically put yourself into the "Bring It!" mindset is to be exceptionally loud. Think about it: If you were just waking up in the morning and your energy was very low, it would be very difficult to start yelling at the top of your lungs, right? So, the opposite must be true. Force yourself to be AS LOUD AS POSSIBLE during practice and games.

When you do this, you will spike your intensity level and feel much more activated, focused, and ready to stop the ball. Being loud in the cage is a tangible way to change your physiology to a more prepared, aggressive mindset.

You must practice implementing the "Bring It!" mindset as much as possible. Changing from a fearful mindset to aggressive one is very difficult to do, but it's not impossible. Work with a goalie or mental coach and try to get past the negative reactions to fear so that you can focus on what's appropriate – the release point of each shot and making the stop without interference.

Recap:

- You can change your mindset from fearful to confident.
- Technique is not as important as your desire to stop the ball.
- Cultivate a "Bring It!" mindset – daring the other team to shoot on you.
- You must be in the "Bring It!" mindset every time you are in the cage – from practice warm-ups to games.

CHAPTER 6

Mental Toughness

D
r. Robert Harmison, of James Madison University, taught me so much about the essentials of Mental Toughness during grad school. Mental Toughness is a natural and learned psychological edge that allows athletes to "generally cope better than their opponents with the many demands of their sport (e.g. training, competition, lifestyle), remaining determined, focused, confident, and in control under pressure."

Here are 10 components to mental toughness as it applies to lacrosse goalies:

1.) Personal Standards

— Mentally tough athletes compete against their own standards of performance.

In order to be mentally tough, you must learn to judge your performances by your own standards. This means you need to understand when you do well relative to what you have been working on, not versus other players.

For example, let's say you've been playing JV all year. At the end of the season, you get called up to finish the year with the varsity during the playoff season. During that first practice with varsity, it may be very difficult to keep up with the speed of the shots by the older varsity players. Mentally tough goalies recognize this. They recognize that this environment is new. It's faster. There is going to be an adjustment period. Cut yourself some slack if you can't keep up at first.

Mentally tough athletes don't measure their standards versus somebody else's. Just because the goalie on the other team is playing well, there is no reason to compare his performance to yours. If that goalie is an All-American, good for him. It has nothing to do with you or your performance.

Focus on your own standards. For example, if you are putting in a new arc, or holding your hands in a new position, recognize that your performance may dip while you make those changes. Tiger Woods knows something about focusing on his own standard. He changed his swing while he was #1 in the world… twice!

2.) Unquenchable Desire

– Mentally tough athletes possess a strong, internal desire to succeed.

The idea of this "Unquenchable Desire" goes to the first level of the Lacrosse Hierarchy, which we will discuss later on. You must possess the internal drive to improve in order to rise to the level of lacrosse you desire. Mentally tough goalies are ALWAYS looking to improve and succeed. Which means, if you put in the extra time before or after practice and in the off-season, continuously trying to improve your skills, you will set yourself apart from the other goalies who aren't willing to go that extra mile.

Also, notice that in the definition, it says an "internal" desire to succeed. If you're mentally tough, awards or praise does not motivate you, but rather by feeling proud of the hard work you have put in. You see value in hard work. You are motivated by something inside you that always wants you to do your best and put in the extra effort.

3.) Unshakable Belief

– Mentally tough athletes possess an unshakable belief in their ability to achieve their goals.

The key word here is "unshakable." Even when times are tough and you don't think you can save a beach ball, you still believe in yourself chalk it up to a bad day. Even the best goalies in the world that I have worked with have all gone through tough times. But they trust it will not last forever, and it is just a temporary phase. You have to believe, deep down inside, no matter what, you will achieve your goals. Choose to think that way and cultivate that feeling so it is undeniable.

Optimally, you want to reach a point where no matter what the circumstance, your belief in your own abilities is unshakable. For example, I once asked a NCAA freshman goalie the night before his first college start against the #2 team in the country, "So, how are you going to sleep tonight?" "Like a baby," he said. Now, that is an unshakable belief in oneself.

4.) Unique Strengths

> *– Mentally tough athletes believe that they possess unique strengths that make them better than their opponents.*

This is one I see often, but not enough goalies capitalize on it. Recognize the things that make you unique. What is different about your technique?

Your communication? Your outlet passes? What makes you different from all other goalies. Mentally tough goalies know there are certain things about their play that is like nobody else - and they take pride in that, rather than feel self-consciousness about it.

5.) Dogged Determination

- Mentally tough athletes bounce back from set-backs with optimism and hope.

We all know those players who consistently have a great attitude no matter their situation. Why is that? The answer: I'm not sure. What is it that makes a player constantly optimistic, that no matter what happens, they know that everything will work out? It's possible that just comes naturally to them, but you can also *learn* to be that way.

Self-talk occurs whenever athletes think to themselves or out loud. It consists of interpretive and content-specific verbalizations or statements addressed to the self, is multi-dimensional and dynamic in nature, and serves both instructional and motivational functions for the athlete (Hardy, 2006). You can improve your performance by using positive self-talk that encourages, praises, and is optimistic. Examples may be,

"I've got this," "I am good," "I can best any shooter on any team!"

On the other hand, negative self-talk is critical, creates doubt, and is irrational. I often run into athletes who say very negative things to themselves, like "You suck!" "You're choking!" "You've never played so badly!" And I understand why we say those things to ourselves, but I ask you this: Would you ever say those things to a friend or teammate? Probably not. So say positive things to yourself like, "Concentrate," "Focus on the release," "You've got this," "Let it go," etc. and at least treat yourself as well as you would a teammate or friend.

6.) Present Focus

– Mentally tough athletes remain fully focused on the task at hand in the face of distractions.

As discussed earlier, distractions can be both internal and external. Internal distractions are anything forcing you to lose focus that originates from inside the body. Internal distractions can be both physical or psychological, or both. Psychological distractions can be the pressure of having to play well, somatic anxiety, mental chatter (where your mind races with a dozens of irrelevant thoughts), a previous poor play, impressing your coach (or your girlfriend - let's face it, it happens), impressing potential college coaches, etc. All of these circumstances can effect you psychologically, taking your focus away from what is necessary in order to play well.

Internal physical distractions, on the other hand, can be nagging injuries you're still not sure about, returning from a serious long-term injury, and/or worry about yet another concussion. You can see how your physical distractions can easily start to become psychological distractions - and around and around we go...

External distractions can be anything from away fans, home fans, refs, the condition of the field or the facility, the bus ride to a far away game, the weather, etc.

Remember, mentally tough athletes remain focused on the task at hand no matter the distractions. Your goal is to remain completely focused on the release point and the contact point with an aggressive attitude throughout the game.

7.) Mental Control

– *Mentally tough athletes regain mental control following uncontrollable events.* "*Control the controllables.*"

We will talk about this more in the chapter "Getting off the bench," but for now recognize that if you want to be mentally tough you must learn to control the controllables. What can you control? In simple terms, your thoughts and your actions.

I often see athletes trying to control things that are out of their control. Trying to control something outside of your control is called "suffering." You cannot control your playing time. (But you can influence it). You cannot control the league you play in. You cannot control your teammates or their level of play. You cannot control the refs.

If you want to be mentally tough, you must focus on controlling the things you can. Control your emotions. Control your reactions to a bad play. Control how much you prepare. Control how hard you work in your practice warm-up or individuals with your coach. Control how much film you watch to prepare for each game. Simplify your approach to the position by focusing on the controllables. Let go of controlling anything outside yourself.

8.) Competitive Anxiety

— Mentally tough athletes accept competitive anxiety and know they can cope with it.

There are dozens of anxiety disorders that exist for the average person: Post Traumatic Stress Disorder, Panic Disorder, Obsessive-Compulsive Disorder, Social Anxiety Disorder, General Anxiety Disorder and specific phobias. Symptoms in most of these disorders include feelings of panic and unease, uncontrollable obsessive thoughts, cold or sweaty hands, shortness of breath, an inability to remain calm, increased heart rate, and muscle tension, to name a few. People will spend hours working with clinical professionals developing the skills necessary to cope with these disorders.

Athletes in a competitive situation can experience the same symptoms as someone suffering from the earlier-mentioned disorders. The ten players stepping onto the court of the NCAA Final Four will experience the exact symptoms that someone suffering from an anxiety disorder will feel: Increased heart rate, shortness of breath, sweaty palms, etc. But, would you trade the opportunity to play on the biggest stage in college basketball like the Final Four?

Mentally tough athletes embrace the nerves that accompany competition. Tiger Woods and Michael Jordan have both said they have never played in competition where they didn't feel nervous. Pretty amazing considering they may be considered the best of all time at their particular sport. The difference is they accept and embrace those nerves.

Think about it. Isn't it why we play sports in the first place? To get to the championship? It makes you feel alive! It's what you have worked so hard for. It's almost a privilege to feel those symptoms of anxiety. And it doesn't necessarily pertain exclusively to the "Big Stage." It can be in any game of the season, or even practice.

Embrace competitive anxiety. Trust that your practice has reinforced that you know what to do. Enjoy the heightened feelings competition brings because you know you can handle it.

9.) Performance Pressure

– Mentally tough athletes thrive on the pressure of competition.

Similar to accepting competitive anxiety, pressure can be seen in the same way. Pressure is a very interesting concept. You can't show me a box of pressure. Pressure is often experienced as a compelling or constraining influence on the mind, or an urgent demand that must be met. But I want you to think about it for a second. What is the "demand" that must be met? And where does it come from?

The perceived "demand" is that you must play well to win, impress your coach, impress potential college coaches, keep your starting spot, have your teammates like you... But, all of those demands are of your own making. When you focus too much on results (performing well), you lose focus on what it is that you have to do in order to play your best. Until you focus on the process and not the results, you will not consistently play your best.

Pressure is a feeling that is created by ourselves when we react to particular events or situations. So, if YOU have placed those demands on yourself, YOU can also change them. Convince yourself to love the pressure of competition.

10.) Push Through Limits

– Mentally tough athletes push through limits and give a little bit more when stressed.

Self-created limitations are one of the biggest obstacles when it comes to improving. Many young athletes create self-limitations that are much lower than what is realistic. I have heard so many times, "I can't do that." Can you bench 185? Can you run a sub-5:00 mile? Can you make 20 saves in one game? Can you make All-American? "No, not me." But why not?

Mentally tough athletes look to push through limitations. One of the most mentally tough athletes

I have ever worked with would constantly push himself, every day, no matter the task. He would win every sprint. (When's the last time you tried that?) He would run track in the winter to improve his speed. He played football and was captain of a state championship team. He was in the weight room almost every day. He literally would push himself every single day. He went on to play at a top 10 DI lacrosse program, which was not surprising because he did what was necessary in order to play lacrosse at the highest level.

So, what will limit you? Can you make 20 saves by the middle of 2nd half without starting to doubt yourself and think, "Can I really keep this up?" If you have a tendency to create self-limitations, you will be uncomfortable when you are playing really, really well. "This isn't like me. I'm sure I'll let some in during the 4th quarter." Or, "I can't be the starter, I'm not good enough." Do not doubt yourself. Do not create limitations. Stay focused on the next shot and just add up the number of stops at the end of the game.

There are obviously many aspects to being mentally tough. Go back through the list above and give yourself a 10 if you are very mentally tough and a 1 if you think it's a major weakness. Once you go through the whole list, make note of your strengths and weaknesses. Then, work everyday on one of your weaknesses until you make it a strength. Your weaknesses will not just disappear. You have to put energy into converting them to strengths. The more you do, the better results you will see.

Recap:

- Mental toughness is the act of remaining determined, focused, confident, and in control under pressure.
- Mental toughness can be learned.
- There are 10 different components to becoming mentally tough.
- You do not need to focus on all 10 components. Learn one or two new skills to boost mental toughness in general.
- Learning to be mentally tough can increase your confidence, help you push through personal limits, remain focused on the task at hand, and perform well under pressure in any given situation.
- Go through each category and rate yourself on each one. Find out your weaknesses then make them your strengths.

CHAPTER 7

The Lacrosse Hierarchy

Improvisation
and Creativity

Mastery of Skills

Composure

Game Scenarios (Rides/Clears)

Understanding Team Offense/Defense

Position-based Fundamentals

Passing/Catching/Ground Balls

Work Ethic / Desire

I put together this model (with the help of a close friend who is also a lacrosse coach) to help athletes identify their level of development in lacrosse and instruct them how to move up from one level to the next.

This model represents all of those who play lacrosse, from beginner to NCAA Division I. It is not simply relative to your situation. Let me explain.

If you would like to play at the highest level, you need to be extremely proficient in all of the areas on this chart. If you wish to play DI lacrosse, I'd say you have to at least reach the "Composure" level to make an impact on the college level. Let's break it down:

Work Ethic / Desire

You cannot be your best self if you don't have the work ethic and desire to improve beyond your current capabilities. It takes SO MANY hours of practice in order to play at the next level. At this point, you have to ask yourself if you have the desire to do what it takes to become your absolute best. And BE HONEST with yourself. That honesty will help you figure out how far you want to take your lacrosse career. You cannot move to the next level of the pyramid without the desire to be your best.

One way to assess your work ethic/desire is to define your motivation. What makes you want to improve? Why do you even play? If the motivation for playing well is attention, awards, and recognition from others, you would be regarded as being ego-oriented. If this is your motivation, you are in for a roller coaster ride as most of those rewards are out of your control like whether or not you win, or whether you receive attention. Even if you play well, you may still not be happy if you did not receive the accolades you were looking for.

One example would be a game where you play exceptionally well, but your team loses nonetheless. In this scenario, you may not get the recognition from your coach, teammates, or parents about your personal performance. Take note of this. Obviously, you would be upset due to your team's loss, but be careful not to get upset because YOU are not getting the accolades about YOUR good play. Be satisfied that you played well, it just may be that your offense may not have been able to put the ball in the back of the net.

Motivation

Ego-orientation means you judge your achievement relative to others. There may be games where you play really well, but the other goalie played even better. It is important to recognize when you played well - especially when you have been working on something new in your technique. If you stopped 75% of the shots on cage, and your team loses, recognize that it was a good game (for you) and move on.

Ego-orientation also means your drive is to improve your social status and build your ego. I have worked with many back-up goalies who feel 'less than' simply because they are the back-up. If you are motivated to improve on the field and become the starter simply so you can feel better about yourself and how others view you, recognize the idea of improving your social status is out of your control. Be confident and realistic with your role.

Lastly, your motivation is ego-oriented if poor performances lead to embarrassment or anger. A bad day in the cage will stick with you for a couple days. When you do play poorly, is your reaction one of anger that you outwardly express – making certain that everyone knows you are much better than that? "I've never played so bad!" is something I hear often from ego-oriented athletes. If you react this way, it will impede your ability to cope with a bad day in the cage, look at what really went wrong with your play, and challenge your self-concept.

A better type of motivation is called Mastery Orientation where the focus is on learning and mastering the task at hand. When you become more mastery oriented, your focus is on YOUR play, and improving, not what others think of you or how you measure up.

Your standards for excellence are self-imposed and self-judged. Start to judge your performances on how YOU did. Did you put in that new stance? Were you able to keep your hands in the right position? Were you able to overcome the fear and combat the urge to shrink in the cage before a shot?

Mastery-oriented athletes consistently work at refining their skills for no other reason but to master the task in front of them. If you play poorly, let it motivate you back to practice and work on whatever wasn't working that day. Get curious, not mad, about the areas of your game that didn't hold up on a particular day and then set your mind to improving them.

Passing / Catching / Ground Balls

Of course having skill in passing, catching, and ground balls is important. But, what we are talking about here is being absolutely proficient at all of these. Not only should you be able to pass and catch with both hands - but you need to be completely competent with both your left and right, be able to catch an awkward pass from a teammate with your off-hand, and get a ground ball in a crowd.

This goes for goalies as well. Being proficient with your off-hand will set you apart from others at showcases or tryouts. Also, many goalies try to get away with what I call the "Catapult" pass. This is where you keep your shoulders facing your target, put your top hand (or dominant hand) on your shoulder, and "push" it towards your teammate.

Instead, turn your shoulders back and through to make a good strong pass. If you want to get to the next level of lacrosse, you must keep working on your stick skills. The minute you think you're good enough, you're not. I worked with a goalie that used to use the "catapult" but he worked really hard on his outlet passes, and now he has perfect outlets.

Matt Danowski (one time NCAA All-time Points Leader) once told me that he played wallball every day before practice and games throughout his college career. So, if he's doing it, don't you think you should too?

Position-Based Fundamentals

This level represents the typical goalie coaching you receive. This includes form, technique, hand speed, hand/eye coordination, your arc, knowing the rules about the crease, etc. If you want to be proficient in this level of the model, you have to constantly refine your skills. Work on your angles. Perfect them. If you want to be the best goalie you can be, you need to continuously improve your form and technique. Even the best goalies in the game constantly work on these areas.

Understanding Team Offense And Defense

This is where you go to the next level as a goalie. If you want to play at the highest level, you must learn the team's defense (and offense!). While you're in the crease during a six-on-six, you need to know what every player on your defense should be doing. You have to know how to run a defensive zone. You are the quarterback, the assistant coach, and the defensive coordinator all at once. Pay attention during practice.

Furthermore, you must understand team OFFENSE. Yeah, that's right, the offense. To move up this ladder, you need to know what offenses are going to do against your zone so that you will know whom and where the shooters will be. It will make you a better goalie and allow the coach to depend on you.

Game Time Scenarios

Game time scenarios are all the aspects of the game that are specific to that game. How are you going to clear the ball this week? What type of ride is appropriate? How will you run your man-down defense?

At the highest levels of lacrosse, it is not enough anymore to just stop the ball. You have to know how to clear the ball correctly. Top college programs clear the ball 95% of the time. You must know how to orchestrate a clear, and a ride for that matter. No excuses.

You must also completely understand how your man-down defense works for all offensive formations (3-3, 2-3-1, 2-2-2, etc.). You want the defense to put the shooters in spots you feel most comfortable (i.e. making the shooter shoot with his off-hand). It is also your job to read the scouting report (if you have them) and know exactly what your opponent's offense runs on man-up. Remember, if you have the desire and work ethic, you will take the extra time to learn all about the opposing team's tendencies in your upcoming game.

Composure

So now you have all the fundamentals down, and you have reached a level of performance you didn't think possible. At this level of the pyramid it's time to talk about the mental part of playing the game.

The definition of composure is "the state or feeling of being calm and in control of oneself." I would say it is almost impossible to have composure in a game if you have not fully mastered the lower levels of this pyramid. If your angles and form are not groomed to perfection, they will break down if you are not composed.

When we get nervous, we relapse back to our old bad habits, so to be poised under pressure, perfect the fundamentals. The key to good fundamentals, and ultimately composure, is to work on them every day. Really work on them. Go out early and get shots from a teammate or coach. Work on very specific components of your game by having a plan before you go out to practice. Just mindlessly taking shots will only allow you to improve so much. Have a plan.

Once you are in the game, trust that your hard work has paid off. To have composure, you must feel that you are in control. You must feel that the practice time you have put in is enough. Don't try to improve during the game, just play. Find the release and trust yourself. (We will talk more about confidence later on.)

Mastery Of Skills / Improvisation And Creativity

Here we are talking about the crème-de-la-crème of goaltending. Players on this level are the best of the best. They are the ones who can stop any shot; can run their defense like an army general; can try new and different techniques and master them quickly. These guys can be a one-man clear but can also run the 3-across clear like a machine. This level is for the goalies that make the incredible saves - all the time! At this level, you need to think outside the box. What is best about your play? How can you change the entire game? Heck, how can you change how the position is played and change the sport as a whole?!

There are no limitations when you are at this level. Nothing is out of your reach. No shot too fast. You are out-thinking the shooters before they even shoot. You have read the scouting report to know all the shooters' tendencies. This is the level where it all comes together in perfect harmony where the lacrosse ball looks like a beach ball and the game seems like it's in slow-motion. I hope you reach this level where only a very small number of goalies have played…so far.

No matter where you fall on this pyramid, realize that only hard work will move you up to the next level. Ask your coach what level of the pyramid he or she believes you are on. They will give you an honest evaluation of your level of play. But remember, you must be open to the criticism because only then can you make changes and experience growth. Once you have an idea of what level you are on, figure what you need to do to advance to the next level on the pyramid. Work hard each day to improve.

We all want to be All-American, but it is only those who are willing to put in the work that actually earns it.

Recap:

- You must work on strengths and weaknesses in order to move up the talent pyramid.
- Work ethic and desire are absolute necessities if you want to improve.

- You must be proficient at each level before you can move on the next. (Yes, that means passing and catching lefty.)
- You must learn team defense AND offense. It will only make you a better goalie and leader.
- Composure is the key level for you to aspire to. The only way to do that is to work hard on the fundamentals.

CHAPTER 8

Taking Responsibility

Responsibility = Response Ability
- RICHARD INNES

"Coach, it's not my fault. The defense didn't slide." This phrase, or something close to it, is what goalies say when they are trying to save face after letting up a goal. Even if they don't say it, they think it.

Goalies (including myself back in the day) yell at their defense immediately after the ball goes in the goal. I believe this is a personal defense mechanism. The goalie who does this is trying to release all responsibility of doing their job of stopping the ball by blaming the defense instead. It is much easier to blame others than to take responsibility and admit it was your fault.

But here's the thing: It IS your fault. No matter what. After all, you did let it in. I understand the odds may be against you at times. Heavily against you. But even if you are three men down, it is your responsibility to stop the ball, regardless of the situation.

I see this almost every time there is a broken clear. For example, you are working really hard to get the ball upfield and into the offensive zone, you make a perfect pass to your defenseman and he drops it. The other team scoops it up, and the play ultimately ends up with you facing an attackman who is all alone, one on one.

The broken clear is not your fault. If the shot goes in on a 1-on-1, so what? You weren't supposed to make it anyway; especially considering it was a 1-on-1 with the goalie. What really happens is that you give up before the attackman even shot it because you are upset about the dropped pass. Stop the ball. Help out your defenseman for his mistake. It obviously wasn't his intention to drop the ball on the clear.

Take responsibility for ALL shots that go in. Goalies tend to blame a goal on anything but themselves. They tend to divert blame for shots that elude them due to poor defense, unlucky bounces, backside feeds, etc. You are the goalie. It is your job to make stops, no matter the circumstances.

Only when you take responsibilities for all shots/goals can you make the appropriate adjustments. By taking responsibility, you have the ability to respond how you want. Taking responsibility allows you to separate the word into two words: Response ability. The ability to respond however you like. Think about it: If a goal is never your fault, you would never need to make any changes to correct mistakes. Also, your defense will respect you more for it.

If you deflect blame to everyone else, you will cause frustration and tightness. It can be difficult to take constructive criticism. Own the reason for each goal and respond accordingly. You missed it. Big deal. Choose to release the last shot and move on the next one.

You must take responsibility for all shots. It is your job to stop the ball. No more yelling at the defense if you let one in. If you save it, well that's a different story.

Recap:

- It is your responsibility to stop all shots, no matter difficult the circumstances.
- If you take responsibility for your actions, you can change it into two words: Response Ability
- Responsibility = Response ability. Only when you have taken responsibility can you respond in a way that will make you great; never blame your teammates.

CHAPTER 9

Anxiety

Your team is up 10 – 7 in the fourth quarter. With three minutes to go in the game, you let one get past you. 10 - 8. After the ensuing face-off, their face-off middie comes right down the middle, no one slides, and he puts in another. 10 – 9, with just over two minutes to go in the game...

It is possible that your team wins the next face-off and closes out the game with a one-goal victory. But, what if the other team wins the next face-off? Their coach may very well call a timeout as they take it onto your side of the field. What are you thinking? What are you going to do?

This is an example of a time when goalies can become tight and nervous or experience what we in the sport psychology world call a "high state of anxiety." There are many other examples of typical high anxiety situations: State championships, rival games, showcases, tryouts, your first start, etc. It doesn't matter what the scenario may be. What is important is that you recognize WHEN you are experiencing high levels of anxiety.

The most important aspect of coping with anxiety is being aware of it in the first place. You must recognize your reaction to anxiety, which is characterized by a presence of recognizable unpleasant feelings of intensity, preoccupation, disturbance, and apprehension. Another way to think of it is "getting nervous, or tight."

A high state of anxiety can occur when we have negative expectations and negative evaluations of ourselves, the situation at hand, and the consequences. Let's go back to the example: At the end of a close game, we may encounter negative thoughts doubting our ability to make a save in those last few moments. As a goalie, we know it all comes down to you. Can you stop them from scoring? Do you have the ability to handle any situation they throw at you?

You can reduce the frequency of experiencing high levels of anxiety by increasing your confidence, but I will explain that later. For now, I want to focus on what symptoms to look for when we are in a high state of anxiety.

In order to recognize you are experiencing a higher level of anxiety, you must first be able to identify the symptoms. You will notice a general sense of nervousness and you will feel your heart rate increase. Your muscles will tighten (most noticeably your shoulders, arms, hands, and neck), and your breathing rate will decrease by taking shorter, shallower breaths. You will sweat more, and your digestive system might even start to shut down (that's the "butterflies" you may feel in your stomach).

You have to recognize when you are having these physiological responses. Without diagnosing these reactions, you can't change them. But now that you have identified them, you CAN begin to adjust those responses by relaxing your shoulders, loosening your grip, taking deep breaths, etc.

I have worked with goalies that intensely move toward the ball in "big" games because they are nervous. They throw everything they have at each shot. They crouch down and explode towards the ball. This might sound like a good idea, but all week during practice they stand taller, waiting for the release, their hands are quicker, and they save everything coming their way.

Often, what that is is a anxious response to an impending shot. You get so wound up that you move before the ball is even in the air.

So here's a tip: Try putting a little more weight on your heels. It forces you to stand tall, not crouch down so much and sit on the release a little longer. It will help you remain more relaxed so you can focus on the release. Some goalie coaches will say I'm crazy – "You should always be on the balls of your feet" – not always...

Try moving your weight to your heels and see what happens. Experiment. Figure out what works for you. Talk to your goalie or mental coach about what your tendencies are and then WORK ON THEM! They won't magically go away unless you address the problems.

Some goalies need to make a save early to feel as though they are "into" the game. Let's say you let in the first two shots you see. A goalie that tends to rely on making saves early in order to have a good game is leaving himself open to circumstance. What if the first two shots are from 4 or 5 yards out, on a fast break and no defense?

So you let the first two in and stop the next 8... Would you take an 80% save percentage? That means if you let in the first two, you CAN make the next 8. You've done it before. But I'll tell you this, if you think you have to save the first couple of shots to have a good game, and you don't make those saves, it is almost impossible to play well after that if you think you CAN'T turn it around. Recognize and admit that you're feeling nervous.

Another key to dealing with performance anxiety is to embrace the nerves you get before games, like we talked about earlier. If you didn't get nervous before games, it could mean that you don't care. But you do care. So embrace the situation. You could be home on the couch, right?

If are experiencing high levels of anxiety during a game or warm-up, try to slow down and take long, deep breaths. This will slow down your heart rate and loosen your muscles. Try to control the mental chatter you may experience by focusing on very few things, like the ball. Slow down. Relax. Chill. Wait on the ball... And remember, the more you prepare, the higher your confidence, and the lower your anxiety.

Recap:

- You can feel anxiety in many different situations on and off the field.
- Recognize the symptoms of anxiety: Shortness of breath, fast hear rate, excessive sweating, muscular tension.
- Embrace the anxiety. It's why you play in the first place.
- Put more weight on your heels and wait on the release. Anxiety can force you to step even before the ball is in the air.

CHAPTER 10

The Downward Spiral

"Fear *can change your entire perspective, and worse, it institutes a downward spiral that re-supplies its own strength. [Athletes] with lower self-efficacy who interpret physiological arousal as fear produce more of a stress hormone called norepinephrine whose job is to tense the muscles,*" says Dr. Gio Valiante, author of Fearless Golf, (p. 36).

As an athlete's self-efficacy dips, they can go into a "downward spiral." (Self-efficacy is a person's belief in their ability to perform a task.) During that downward spiral, fear *"feeds on itself and triggers the sympathetic nervous system to do two key things… First, norepinephrine is produced and muscles tense up. Second, capillaries in the hands constrict, making [athletes] lose feeling in their hands such that their grip becomes really tight."*

So, what Dr. Gio is saying is that once you feel a sense of fear, a whole bunch of chemicals will be introduced into your body by the brain. This will restrict the goalie's ability to stay relaxed and stop the shot. Not making stops can decrease self-efficacy and increase fear, and "the *cycle simply repeats and insidiously feeds on itself over and over*" (p.37).

Let's put this in straight lacrosse goalie terms: The Downward Spiral is when you let in a couple of goals (without making any saves), then another, and so on, and so on... you get the picture. We all know that feeling where we just want to make one save to break out of the current slump.

Remember, the next shot is ALWAYS more important than the last one. Your attention needs to be on the release point of the NEXT shot, not the save you just made. If you have the tendency to think that you need to make the first save to get into the flow of the game, try to change it. There is absolutely no value in thinking; "I'll be fine after I make that first save."

By thinking that way, you actually encourage the downward spiral. If you need to make that first save (in your mind) and you don't, what happens when you let in two in a row, or three, or four? The pressure will just start to build. Let's say you don't make a save in the entire first half, then what?

I was fortunate to be working with a goalie that had an extraordinary turn of events happen to him during a game. He was playing one of the best teams in the nation. His team seemed to be prepared before the game, but once the game started, his whole team looked scared and seemed to be playing to not lose, rather than to win. (And his team was nationally ranked in the Top 10 at the time.)

He let in 9 goals in the first half. This was not normal for a goalie of his caliber (he is considered one of the best in the country.) As he was walking towards me at halftime, I said to him, "You're hands are stuck to your chest," meaning that he was playing scared and in a fearful position. He exclaimed in frustration, "THEY ARE COMPLETELY STUCK TO MY CHEST!" ...I guess I didn't have to tell him.

As he took the field in the second half, reciting the phrase "Bring it" over and over in his head. His whole demeanor changed. His head was much higher. His hands were way out in front of him. He moved better. He must have made 12 saves in that second half.

What's great about this story is that in the future he can always go back to this game and remember that he climbed his way out of the downward spiral. He made the correction physically AND mentally. He recognized he was playing scared and made the adjustment. In the first half he was worried about losing, but in the second half he was focused on winning, the release point and committing to stopping the shot. He wanted them to shoot. He dared them to shoot. "Bring It!"

Recap:

- Don't let yourself slide into the downward spiral.
- The downward spiral is based on momentum. (We don't bank on momentum).
- Recondition your mind to always focus on the next shot so you never allow the downward spiral to begin.
- Forget about making that 'first save.' There is no value in thinking about it that way.
- Be mentally prepared for the first shot. Find the release. It goes in, or it doesn't.

CHAPTER 11

The Warm-Up

The Pre-Practice Warm-Up

If you're like me, there was very little time during practice for actually working on, and improving, your technique. As a coach, I know it is important, but it's really difficult to get the time during the season to focus on each position. So the best time to work on your technique is every day before practice during your warm-up. That should give you at least 15 minutes a day to improve your form. (That is almost two hours a week dedicated to enhancing your talent.)

Your practice warm-up MUST HAVE A PURPOSE. It is imperative that you work on some specific area you need to improve, like stick plane, moving your hands away from your body, movement to the ball, keeping your angles square to the shooter, or finding the release and contact point. The possibilities are literally endless.

But make sure that you are working on something, anything, during your warm-up.

When you start your warm-up, take 20 to 30 shots to simply get warm. Sometimes I'll do a "Warm-up warm-up" where the shooter will take 40 to 50 easy shots all over the cage from a close distance. This simply warms up your muscles and gets your brain programmed to focus on the ball/release.

After you are warm, start working on your technique. Have the shooter start to pick up the speed of each shot. Some goalies like to start with the 6 spots on cage with about ten to twelve shots in each spot (Top Right, Top Left, Stick-side Hip, Off-side Hip, Stick-side Low, Off-side Low, and bouncers). Instead, when I warm up goalies, I like to break the goal into thirds: Top Third, Middle Third, and Lower Third.

Have the coach or player warming you up shoot 10-20 shots at the top third of the goal. Then, when you're ready, move to the middle section, then to the lower third of the goal (from your knees to your feet), and finally finish with bounce shots. The reason I shoot anywhere in each third is because you will never know where the shooter is going to shoot (unlike ten shots or so to each of the six traditional locations). So why not practice finding the release and contact point during the warm-up? To me, shooting in random places is more realistic.

(Note: Practice doesn't make perfect, PRACTICE MAKES PERMANENT. So make sure you are warming up with the right technique and intensity. If you take your warm-up lightly, treating it like just another drill, you will play that way all the time. It's how the brain works. Practice as if you were playing in a game with the same intensity and energy.)

After you have seen shots in each third of the cage and bouncers, and now that you have really warmed up the body, eyes, and mind, it's time to see some serious shots. When coaching varsity or college goalies, I know that I can no longer shoot at the speed you are going to see in a game. Heck, I was a goalie, not a middie. So, I like to have the best shooter on my team shoot ten to fifteen shots anywhere he wants but as hard as he can. This will allow you to be prepared for the upcoming practice or game where you will see all kinds of shots at different speeds and locations.

One of my goalies really took his warm-up to the next level. After he received some shots just to warm up, he would turn and face the goal and not turn back again until he was ready and completely focused and ready for the next save. He would make the save, throw it back to the shooter, then turn and face the goal again, preparing for the next one. He would repeat this routine for every shot. He was making sure that he made each save as though he were in a game.

During the warm-up, too many goalies just make the save and quickly throw the ball back to the coach shooting on him, just to get another shot immediately after that. Take your time in between shots towards the end of your warm-up. This particular goalie may only take 6 to 10 shots per minute because he spends so much time in between shots preparing for the next one. He is now playing for a NCAA national championship team.

So, make your warm-up counts. Every day. Get better every day. Work hard to improve during practice and make sure your warm-up is part of that process.

Before the Pre-Game Warm-Up

If you are serious about playing your absolute best, you must mentally prepare before each game. But what does that mean?

All athletes have an ideal zone for optimal performance. This means that there is a mental state that is best for peak performance. You must learn what that optimal mental state is for you. Are you fired up? Relaxed? Anxious? Confident? Focused? Loose?

First figure out what mindset works best for you to play your absolute best. Then 15 to 30 minutes BEFORE YOU GET ON THE FIELD, you must start to get into that optimal mindset. Create a routine

or behavior that you use ca
mindset. That is called a t
be when you are putting o
imagine that you are a gla
into the arena for battle. Ai
to a set of songs on your il
field that pumps you up (or pumps you down if that's
the case). Using a trigger will help you get into the
right mindset before you start your warm-up.

Pre-Game Warm-Up

Your game day warm-up is similar to the practice
warm-up. You want to start by simply warming up
your muscles, but before a game, you should NOT
focus on any technique improvements or adjustments
to your form. That was what practice was for. Now
it is time for you to just play. Rely on the fact that
all your hard work has paid off. You should probably
only see half of the number of shots you would see in
a practice warm-up.

During your pre-game warm-up, once you have
gotten a little warmer in the cage, start focusing on
each individual shot. Put all your attention on committing to each shot. You want to treat this warm-up
as if you were playing in the game. Take your time. It's
not a race. During the pre-game warm-up, it is your
time to get dialed in.

mething unique to this warm-up. I watched
ave two shooters for the goalie towards the
of the starting goalie's warm-up. One coach
ould take a shot, then the other coach would shoot
two to three seconds after the first shot. Imagine that
this would simulate a rebound. It was a great way
to get your intensity and focus to game levels. You
certainly don't have to add this particular exercise
to your warm-up, but add something that is unique
to your warm-up to help you prepare for the game
mentally.

You can also get more prepared for the game by
working on your outlet pass during the warm-up.
Ask one of the back up goalies to stand somewhere
between the restraining line and the mid-line. After
each save, throw an outlet to the back-up. If you
have more than one back-up, ask both of them
to stand out there on opposite sides of the field.
Alternate throwing to each one so you feel that
much more comfortable throwing outlet passes before the game - in a real-life simulation of the impending game.

Recap:

- Every warm-up must have a purpose.
- Make sure to use the warm-up you like, not the
  person warming you up.

- Practice does not make perfect, practice makes permanent so be sure to warm-up everyday like it's game day.
- Create specific pre-practice warm-ups as well as pre-game warm-ups that help you get mentally prepared.

CHAPTER 12

Confidence

In a recent presentation to approximately 75 goalies at the G3 Goalie Camp, we watched a highlight reel of several MLL goalies. After the film, I asked, "So, what did you notice?" One answer was very interesting.

One of the attendees answered that the MLL goalies "looked" confident. That comment struck me. Confidence is an emotion. We can't see emotions. They are not physical. So how could he see confidence? What does confidence look like? What are the characteristics of someone playing confidently?

I believe someone who "looks" confident in the cage is someone who is ready to act, who is aggressively relaxed, who holds their stance longer into the shot after the ball is released, and who sees the ball all the way from release point to contact point. Usually after a save, they will show some form of emotion with a fist pump or something similar. (I believe an emotional response after a save is a release of the all the intensity, focus, and energy necessary to play at the highest level. But I digress...)

How do you play with a higher level of confidence? If you learn how to change your confidence level, then apply it to your play; you can play at levels you never thought possible. But the key here is to APPLY THEM. Confidence does not just happen. It must become a practice. It takes time and energy to apply certain thought processes in order to make the changes you are looking for and see results.

Professional performance coach, Brendon Burchard, believes that confidence is not a myth. He asks his readers to think about a time in life where you have already experienced some sort of confidence. To think about certain times when you felt confident, on or off the field. What do you notice about that feeling of confidence?

We need to understand the foundation of what gave you that feeling. Then learn about the times when you didn't feel so confident and what it was that was holding you back.

Confidence is a belief, as well as a sensation. Confidence is something you generate, which over a period of time, becomes a part of you. Burchard likens it to a power plant. The power plant doesn't have energy. It generates energy. The same can be said for confidence. You need to generate confidence. In other words, you need to purposely condition your mind to have specific confident beliefs.

Confidence is a belief and a feeling that things will turn out well because you are willing, worthy, and capable. Allow yourself permission to feel that you belong. That you are good enough. That you are capable. That you have the knowledge, skill, and talent to pull off the task at hand. Allow yourself permission to feel willing, worthy, and capable of playing well against any team at any time in any game.

Confidence is knowing you can cope, act as you intend, and succeed in any given situation. It's trusting that you will reliably show up as your best self and excel in that situation. For the next 30 days, reliably show up as the best of who you are. Work hard to feel this way the best you can in practice, games, or as individuals.

In order to improve confidence, you must start with things you can control. What can you control when it comes to your performance? If you feel you have no control over your performance, you can feel stressed, overwhelmed, and possibly depressed.

So what do we control when it comes to your play in the cage? Your technique, work ethic, angles, preparation, and mindset are all things we can control while we play. Many athletes think they can control whether or not they start in games. They cannot.

However, you CAN influence your coach by how well you do in the things you can control. Do you stay after practice or show up early to put in the extra work necessary to be prepared? Do you constantly work to improve your angles and technique? Do you watch film to tweak your overall play during games? Focus on the things that you can control and put your all into those things. The more you focus on the things you can control, the more confident you will feel about your actions and behaviors.

Burchard believes competence is another component to increasing your confidence. Competence is the belief you have in your ability to accomplish something. It is the belief that you can master a certain skill. The more competence you have, or belief that you are good at a certain skill, the more confident you will feel.

So to develop more competence, you need to keep working in practice and on your own time to enhance your skills. The more prepared you are at playing the position, the more confident you will feel. Watch film. Watch MLL or NCAA games online or on TV during the season. What is your learning plan? You need to work to increase your level of competence, which will, in turn, increase your confidence. Get it?

Decide to generate confidence on a consistent enough basis so it starts to feel natural. The next time you are playing, decide to think, "I can do this," "I am going to put in my best effort," or "I've got this." Do this over and over, even though it may feel awkward at times. You may feel some fear, but think confidently and trust that you have prepared for that moment. Do not be blocked by fear.

As I said in the beginning of this chapter, it may be possible to "see" confidence. When is comes to looking and feeling confident, a trick you can use is to adjust your physical demeanor (confident body language: shoulders back, chin up, chest out). By simply acting confidently, you will start to feel confident in turn.

Some think you first have to be confident in order to have confident body language, but this is not necessarily the case. The reverse can also be true. Try standing confidently and using confident body language. Try this during warm ups. Stand tall in the cage. Shoulders back. Chin up. You will start to feel confident as well.

Another tangible way to improve confidence is through goal-setting. There are no laws in sport psychology, but if there were, it would be that goal-setting works. Set small, easily-achievable goals for yourself in the short-term. Examples of small goals could be: Stay after practice every day for two weeks and get additional shots for 20 minutes; Play wallball for 15 minutes every day for two weeks; Learn how to juggle; Jump rope every day for 10 minutes before practice or working out.

Make sure that you write these goals down somewhere that you will see them every day. I suggest to my clients that they write them down on a index card then place them in the corner of their bathroom mirror. That way they will see them at least twice a day.

Once you've met those small goals, create new ones. Then once you've met those, make some more. As you go through this exercise and you start meeting all the goals you set for yourself, you'll start to feel more accomplished and more capable. You will start to feel more confident each day in practice or a game.

Recap:

- Confidence is something you generate, which over a period of time becomes a part of you.
- Allow yourself permission to feel that you belong. That you are good enough.
- For the next 30 days, reliably show up as the best of who you are. Work hard to feel this way the best you can in practice, games, or as individuals.
- Competence is the belief you have in your ability to accomplish something. The more competence you have, or belief that you are good a certain skill, the more confident you will feel.

- Try using confident body language as well: Chin up, shoulders back, chest out.
- Set small, achievable goals. Be sure to write them down. If you don't write down goals, they are just dreams.

CHAPTER 13

Reaction Time

Ok, it's time to get a little technical, psychologically speaking. On the following pages are descriptions of experiments that measure reaction time. The goal of playing your best is to react as quickly possible to every shot. By doing this, you improve, or lower/decrease, your reaction time.

This analysis comes from a portion of "A Literature Review on Reaction Time," by Robert J. Kosinski at Clemson University. You can also find it online at http://biae.clemson.edu/bpc/bp/lab/110/reaction. htm#Kinds. I'll try to simplify each study and explain how learning the results of these experiments can help you improve your performance in the cage by improving your reaction time.

Number of possible valid stimuli. Several investigators have looked at the effect of increasing the number of possible stimuli in recognition and choice experiments. Hick (1952) found that in choice reaction time experiments, response was proportional to log(N), where N is the number of different possible stimuli. In other words, reaction time rises with N, but once N gets large, reaction time no longer increases so much as when N was small. This relationship is called "Hick's Law."

Translation: Reaction time gets worse with the increase in number of stimuli. So how does knowing that help you play goalie? If you limit the number of stimuli, you should have quicker reactions. To reduce the number of stimuli (or in this case distractions), focus on just the release point of the ball. By singularly focusing on the release point and contact point without distractions, you will reduce the number stimuli, thus allowing the brain to react quicker.

Type of Stimulus

Many researchers have confirmed that reaction to sound is faster than reaction to light (Galton, 1899; Woodworth and Schlosberg, 1954; Fieandt et al., 1956; Welford, 1980; Brebner and Welford, 1980).

Translation: You will react faster when you HEAR a stimulus, rather than when you SEE one. So how does this help you? It doesn't. Unless they start putting a bell in the ball. Let's move on.

Stimulus Intensity

Froeberg (1907) found that visual stimuli that are longer in duration elicit faster reaction times.

Translation: You need to stay focused as long as possible on the release - or potential release. For example, you can improve your reaction time if you are focused on the ball as soon as a middie starts his dodge from the outside. This allows you to lengthen the preparation time and react faster once the shot is released.

Piéron (1920) and Luce (1986) reported the weaker the stimulus (such as a very faint light) is, the longer the reaction time is. However, after the stimulus gets to a certain strength, reaction time becomes constant.

Translation: If you perceive the shot as intense and thus intensely focus on the ball/release, you will react faster. Treat every shooter the same, with high intensity.

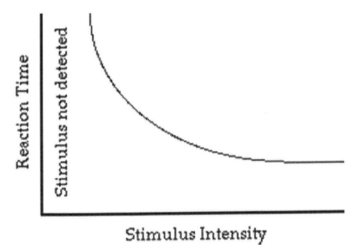

Arousal. One of the most investigated factors affecting reaction time is 'arousal' or state of attention, including

muscular tension. Reaction time is fastest with an interme-diate level of arousal, and deteriorates when the subject is either too relaxed or too tense (Welford, 1980; Broadbent, 1971; Freeman, 1933).

Translation: First of all, "Arousal" is not as excit-ing as it sounds. Arousal, generally speaking, means how intense you are. How aware and alert you are. Being "fired up" or "psyched" would be considered a high level of arousal and being tired and bored would be considered a low level of arousal.

What this data states is there is some level of interme-diate level of arousal that is best for you when reacting to shots. You need to experiment and find out how to find that level. Listening to music before a game or practice is a great way to raise, or lower, your arousal level (i.e., Techno, Classical, Metal, Rock, Hip Hop, Country, etc. can have different effects in changing your intensity level).

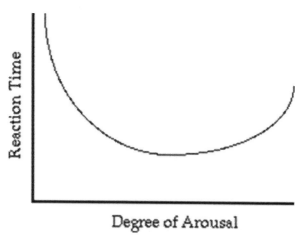

What this graph shows us is that if your arousal level gets too high or too low, it will negatively affect your reaction time. One example of arousal being too low could be when you play a team of perceived lesser skill. We can all recall games when we didn't take that team seriously and were not prepared once the game started. We did not take the time to listen to music, get fired up in pre-game warm-up, and make sure we were ready to play our best, because in our minds, we didn't need to. Make sure you are prepared for every game. Ideally, you should approach each game identically, psychologically speaking. Even better, each shot identically.

There are times where you may be over-aroused. This can happen when you get too nervous. High anxiety will slow down your reaction time. As we discussed, anxiety can tighten your muscles and slow down how quickly you move. If you are too nervous before a game, use long, deep breathing to slow yourself down and calm your nerves. You can also listen to calming music in your warm-up to lower your arousal level before the game starts.

Practice and Errors. *Sanders (1998, p. 21) cited studies showing that when subjects are new to a reaction time task, their reaction times are less consistent than when they have had an adequate amount of practice.*

Translation: If you are new to goaltending, your reaction times will be slower, but with practice, you can react faster. Keep taking shots! Or if you are implementing something new to your technique, like hand position or a wider stance, don't freak out. It will take a little time to adjust to the changes.

Practice and Errors (cont'd). *Also, if a subject makes an error (like pressing the spacebar before the stimulus is presented), subsequent reaction times are slower, as if the subject is being more cautious.*

Translation: Recognize you made a mistake, but stay focused on the task at hand. Every shot is it's own unique stimulus. Condition your mind to consistently focus on the next shot, letting go of the last one.

This can also be seen when goalies step before the ball is even shot. Don't laugh. This happens frequently to most goalies. Goalies see a shot is coming, and get so anxious that they can't wait until the ball is in the air. Watch some MLL goalies' highlight reels. You'll see the ball is three or four feet out of the shooter's stick and they still haven't moved. Wait on the shot. Try not to be cautious. Play to win.

Ando et al. (2002) found that reaction time to a visual stimulus decreased with three weeks of practice, and the same research team (2004) reported that the effects of practice last for at least three weeks.

Translation: You will react more quickly after three weeks of practice. Similarly, your reaction will slow down if you do not practice for three weeks. This means if you put the stick down at the end of season and don't pick it up again until the following pre-season, your reaction time will be slower. Make sure you take some shots in the off-season.

Fatigue. Welford (1968, 1980) found that reaction time gets slower when the subject is fatigued. Mental fatigue, especially sleepiness, has the greatest effect. Van den Berg and Neely (2006) found that sleep deprivation caused subjects to have slower reaction times and to miss stimuli over a test period that lasted two hours.

Translation: Get some sleep! Your reaction time will slow down if you are mentally fatigued, and this study states that sleepiness has the greatest effect. Be sure to get to bed early the night before a game. Also, recognize if you are pulling all-nighters to study for school, your reaction time may suffer.

Distraction. Welford (1980) and Broadbent (1971) reviewed studies showing that distractions increase reaction time. Trimmel and Poelzl (2006) found that background noise lengthened reaction time by inhibiting parts of the cerebral cortex...

Translation: Don't let a loud crowd distract you. If you are playing in a loud arena, focus intently on the release/ball during the game because your reaction times will automatically be altered by the sounds of the crowd. Start focusing during warm-ups. Don't wait until the game starts.

... The effect of distraction may depend on emotional state and prior experiences. Reed and Antonova (2007)

frustrated some subjects by giving them unsolvable problems, and then tested the reaction times of all the subjects with distraction. Subjects who had been given the difficult problems were more slowed and distracted than subjects who had not been frustrated before the reaction time measurement.

Translation: Getting frustrated will only hurt your reaction time. Learn to cope with the situation at hand. Whether you let one in, your defense messed up, or your opponents are too good, stay focused and calm. Your job is to stop the ball and that will take all of your energy and focus. You don't have time for distractions.

Warnings of Impending Stimuli. *Brebner and Welford (1980) report that reaction times are faster when the subject has been warned that a stimulus will arrive soon. Bertelson (1967) found that as long as the warning was longer than about 0.2 sec., the shorter the warning was, the faster reaction time was. This effect probably occurs because attention and muscular tension cannot be maintained at a high level for more than a few seconds (Gottsdanker, 1975).*

Translation: If you are warned of the stimulus before it happens, you will react faster. This is important for goalies to know because you can prepare yourself for the shot. When an attackman is coming around the cage from behind, you know that an impending shot could be coming. Use the ball carrier's dodge as the trigger for you to get hyper-focused on the ball for the shot that is coming. Do not simply wait for the ball to be in the air before you prepare. You must be prepared mentally before the shooter even pulls the stick back to shoot.

Personality Type. *Brebner (1980) found that extroverted personality types had faster reaction times, and Welford (1980) and Nettelbeck (1973) said that anxious personality types had faster reaction times.*

Translation: Anxious and extroverted players have quicker reaction times. This can be good news for those of you who tend to be a little more anxious. The increase in anxiety raises your arousal level and, therefore, allows you to improve your reaction time.

Exercise. *Exercise can affect reaction time. Welford (1980) found that physically fit subjects had faster reaction times, and both Levitt and Gutin (1971) and Sjoberg (1975) showed that subjects had the fastest reaction times when they were exercising sufficiently to produce a heart rate of 115 beats per minute.*

Translation: You are faster when you are exercising and are in good physical shape. Stay activated with a proper warm-up. Take a lap, or two, around the field before you play. You can imagine how difficult it would be to play if you rolled out of bed and immediately jumped in goal. There is no way you could react quickly and perform your best, so make sure you raise your heart rate before playing in practice or games.

Also, there are times when your offense has the ball for an extended amount of time during a game. During that time, your heart rate will lower if you stop moving. Keep active when the ball is at the other end. Keep moving.

If you want to improve your reaction time, get in shape. The goalie finishing last in sprints has become so common that the coaches don't even comment anymore. Get in good physical shape if you want to be faster and more confident.

Punishment, Stress, and Threats. *Shocking a subject when he reacts slowly does shorten reaction time (Johanson, 1922; Weiss, 1965). Simply making the subject feel anxious about his performance has the same effect, at least on simple reaction time tasks (Panayiotou, 2004).*

Translation: Embrace pressure - it will make you faster. These studies state that subjects reacted more quickly when they were worried about their performance. It is commonly said that many of the best athletes became that way because they embraced their nerves and anxiety during competition. It's why we play sports in the first place, right? If you didn't want to feel the nerves of a State Championship, why did you start playing?

Stimulant Drugs. *Caffeine has often been studied in connection with reaction time. Lorist and Snel (1997) found that moderate doses of caffeine decreased the time it took subjects to find a target stimulus and to prepare* *a response for a complex reaction time task. Durlach et al. (2002) found that the amount of caffeine in one cup of coffee did reduce reaction time and increase ability to resist distraction, and did so within minutes after consumption.*

Translation: A cup of coffee before play will improve your reaction time. This does not mean downing a Monster before you play. Too much caffeine can be very dangerous, raising your heart rate to hazardous levels - especially considering you will already be in an excited state due to game or practice situations. But for the older player, digesting caffeine in the equivalent to a cup of coffee will reduce your reaction time.

Recap:

- Reaction time is the time it takes to respond to a stimulus.
- The lower the reaction time, the quicker you will be.
- The longer you stay fixated on the ball and the release point, the faster you will react once the shot is taken.
- Practicing a skill and refocusing on the task at hand after errors will improve your reaction time.

- Internal distractions like fatigue, frustration and anxiety, as well as external distractions like crowd noise and bad weather will poorly effect your ability to react quickly.
- Embracing pressure and exercise will improve your reaction time.

CHAPTER 14

Rods And Cones

The X attackman splits to his right (your left as you face him behind the net) and gets a step past his defender. He sprints to the crease at Goal Line Extended. He wraps around the crease and dunks a finishing shot.

You never saw the ball, and you probably guessed.

This is a typical scenario if you are not trained to focus on the ball once you know the shot is imminent. The key to making stops is to see the release point, but to take it one step further, if you put the ball in the "center" of your vision, you will improve your reaction time.

Direct vs. Peripheral Vision

Brebner and Welford (1980) cite literature that shows visual stimuli perceived by different portions of the eye produces different reaction times.

The fastest reaction time comes when a stimulus is seen by the cones (when the person is looking right at the stimulus). If the stimulus is picked up by rods (around the edge of the eye), the reaction is slower. Ando et al., 2002 found practice on a visual stimulus in central vision shortened the reaction time to a stimulus in peripheral vision, and vice-versa.

The cause of the differences in our visual field is the two different kinds of light receptor cells available in the eye, i.e. the rods and the cone cells. About 94% of the receptor cells in the eye are rods. Rods do not require much light in order to work, however, only provide a blurred and colorless image of our surroundings. For more detailed and clear vision, our eyes are also equipped with light receptor cells called cones which make up about 6% of the total number of light receptor cells in our eyes. While being efficient in providing a clear picture, cones require much more light in order to function. (http://blog.objectiveexperience.com/2010/06/17/how-does-an-eye-tracker-work/)

So, what does all that mean? Well, from this research, we know you will react quickest when the cones of your eyes are focused on the stimulus (the release). Remember, the cones of your eyes focus on only 6% of what you look at.

Try this exercise:

Stare at the "X" below. While staring directly at it (putting the "X" in the center 6% of
your vision), notice how you can still recognize
other items in your vision but only the "X" is
crystal clear.

X

You want to do the same thing with the ball when you
know the shot is coming and all the way to the contact
point.

If you can consistently get the ball and release point
in that 6% of the center of your vision, you will react
faster and make more saves. This would be similar to
the times you were playing and every shot seemed like
it was in slow-motion. It makes sense because you saw
the shot over its entirety (from the exact release point
to contact point).

The next time you start your warm-up in practice,
work really hard at putting the release point in that
center 6% of your vision. After I tried this, I realized
the release point is much further from the shooter's
shooting shoulder than I had expected. I used to look
somewhere around the shoulder and neck area of the
shooter. But, by making sure that I put the exact release
of the shot in that small area picked up by the cones
of the eyes, it became obvious that the release is about
three to four feet away from the shooter's shoulder.

So, especially when shooters are in close, stay fixated on the ball and release point when you know they are going to shoot.

Recap:

- You respond to shots quicker if the release point is in the center 6% of your vision.
- Use your peripheral vision to recognize open players and cutters.

CHAPTER 15

Getting Off The Bench

So, you think you should be getting more playing time. Maybe so, but why aren't you? Question: Can you control the amount of time you play in games?

Sadly, the answer is "No." It is important you realize what you can and can't control in life. You cannot control the amount of playing time you get. If you could, every person on the team would be on the field at all times. And then you'd have 20 people in the box serving 1-minute penalties for too many people on the field, and we don't want that.

The sad truth is that you can't control your playing time, but you can INFLUENCE it. First, you need to recognize the decision for you to play is not up to you, it's up to your coach. But you can influence your coach's decision on whether or not to play you. So, get to know what the coach is looking for, work on those aspects, and you will see the field more.

Let's think about what you can control, what you can influence, and what's out of your control. Things you can control: your thoughts, behaviors, preparation, and reactions. The things you can influence: your coach, teammates, college scouts, your opponents, fans, parents, etc. The things we cannot control: Weather, field conditions, refs, schedule, fans, parents, etc.

You can influence many variables by controlling your thoughts, actions, and reactions. If you know your coach is the gatekeeper of playing time, you have to know why you aren't currently playing and what you need to do to change that.

I have heard countless athletes talk to their coach about playing time and be told exactly what they need to work on in order to get playing time, then do nothing about it. Just talking to the coach is not enough. You have to listen to what he says and take action.

Find out what you need to improve upon and go work on it. Spend 15 minutes before or after practice concentrating on whatever area coach said you need to improve. Work on it every day for at least two weeks, and I guarantee your coach will notice. Would you say you'd be positively influencing your coach at that point?

By controlling your actions and preparation, you can influence your coach. Just by witnessing the extra hard work, your coach will be influenced for the better thus increasing your chances of more playing time. By the way, you also got better during the extra workouts, so you have that going for you, which is nice...

Recap:

You cannot control whether or not you start in a game. Focusing on controlling the controllables in order to play your best and influence the coach to start you.

Things you can control:

- Your Thoughts
- Your Behaviors
- Your Preparation
- Your Attitude

Things you can influence:

- Your Coach
- Teammates
- College Coaches/Scouts
- Opponents
- Fans
- Parents

Things you can't control:

- Being in the starting lineup
- Weather
- Field conditions
- Referees
- Game schedule/Time of play
- Fans
- Parents
- Teammates

CHAPTER 16

Tryouts And Showcases

What is more nerve-wracking, playing in a state playoff game or playing in front of 50 college coaches on the sideline of a summer showcase?

I don't know the answer definitively because everyone will have a different opinion, but I do know the answer isn't obvious. Here is the difference between the two: When playing for your college or high school team, the emphasis is on winning the game and helping your teammates. However, in a showcase, the emphasis is on displaying your talent as an individual.

It is completely normal to feel nervous during a showcase. And why not? You're trying to catch the eye of every college coach in attendance. But that is where the anxiety comes from. You find yourself trying to "perform" for them. And trying to perform rarely works out well in sports.

Can you imagine Tiger Woods or Michael Jordan getting nervous because people were watching? No way. But could you imagine a minor league second baseman getting nervous because there are scouts in the stands? Probably, but that could potentially be the reason why they are in the Minors.

Trying to perform doesn't work. The reason why it doesn't work is because you are focused on what's happening off the field (on the sidelines or in the stands). It is easy to allow your interference to rise when you know every shot you stop or let in could directly affect your entire college future. But what you don't know is that coaches aren't necessarily looking only for saves. As an evaluator at showcases myself, I'm looking for a lot more than that.

Coaches want to see how you react to letting in a goal. Do you slam your stick on the ground? Do you yell at your defense unnecessarily? Or do you simply throw the ball back to the ref and talk to your defense about what happened and how to fix it?

I once asked two goalies to help me back up the cage for warm-ups so I didn't hit any spectators behind the goal with missed shots. They just glanced at me and continued their conversation, ignoring my plea. I asked them a second time, "Do you guys mind helping me out by backing up the cage?" Still, they just looked at me for a second and continued their conversation.

That particular day there were dozens of very talented goalies at the tryout. Those two didn't make the team.

One of the guidelines I ask of my clients is to "Make an Impact" on any showcase or tryout. You can't be wallpaper out there. You have to stand out. Make sure you are loud. Really loud. Be aggressive in your movements and commitment to the ball. Clear the ball with precision, don't just chuck it up field. Go hard in warm ups and line drills. Help the coaches if they ask (or even if they don't).

The difference between the elite athletes and those trying to become one is that the elite athletes ALWAYS try to win. They very rarely try to perform - they just play. By focusing on winning, your energy will be forced into stopping the ball, good clears, and communicating well. Play to win. Go hard for your team. Dominate. Coaches will notice. Trust me.

Recap:

- When playing in showcases and tryouts, don't play to "perform," play to win.
- Stay focused on what is happening on the field, not in the sidelines or stands.

- Play each game like you are playing for your high school team.
- Make sure you make an impact on the game. Be loud. Control the clears. Be fired up mentally. Praise your teammates.
- All your actions matter when you are at a showcase. Coaches are looking for every detail in how you conduct yourself off the field, not just how you played on it.

CHAPTER 17

Putting It All Together

I t's time to put it all together. I think the best way for you to implement the areas we have talked about in this book and improve your mental game is if I give you a practical guide in the form of a timeline.

Off-season (3-6 months before the first practice/game):

In the three to six months before the first day of practice or tryouts, your focus should be on your technique, or your talent. You must work with a coach to figure out what areas of your game need improving. Talent covers many aspects of your game. Areas you should be working on in the off-season are your arc, foot speed, hand speed, overall strength, cardiovascular conditioning, perfecting your angles in the cage, stick skills, as well as any part of the stopping the ball that needs attention, like bounce shots or low-to-high shots, etc.

This period is also the time to work on your confidence. Do not wait until you are in the season to improve your self-efficacy. Just like getting into good physical condition, it takes a while to get into good mental condition as well. Work on your confidence often. Remember, we generate confidence. It doesn't just show up one day.

Be sure to take shots during the off-season. I know it is difficult if you are playing another sport, but you must play wallball every once in a while so that you don't lose all the talent you created during the season. As the scientific studies told us earlier: Your reaction time will slow down if you do not practice a skill within a three week period.

Pre-season (two weeks prior to tryouts):

This is a time where you want to really work on your overall talent. Each day should have high intensity. Work hard and get as much as you can out of each practice. Ask a friend to shoot on you before or after practice. Or both. Get as many reps as you can during this time.

The more shots you get, the higher your confidence will be going into tryouts. This is the time to get comfortable in the cage again after some time away from the game. Be sure to work on the areas your coach addressed during the off-season – because he will be looking for improvement.

If you are a college player, this is the time right before you get back to school. The second half of August is very slow, so be sure to use that time wisely and don't go back unprepared. You want to hit the ground running right from the start.

I see many high school athletes go into college with a mindset of, "I'll get there, get comfortable, find out the rules, and hope it all works out." I suggest to my clients they go in ready to fight for the starting position. Try not to make assumptions about who is starting before you get there. Show up and fight for the spot. Maybe you will start. Maybe last year's starter will get hurt. Who will be the #2 goalie? You? Or, are you just going to see how it goes and maybe start sophomore year? Go for it! Push yourself. Stop the ball every day and get noticed. Your time is now!

Two weeks before tryouts is a time to experiment with your warm-up and make it your own. Try to figure out what level of intensity you want to play with during your warm-up. I suggest going hard right away. That means you need to make sure you are ready to go as soon as you get in the cage. You don't want to ease into it. This is time for energy and intensity. Start to develop your Bring It! mindset right from the start of practice. Remember: Practice makes permanent. So make sure you are practicing like you play in a game. On a scale from 1 to 10, it should be a 9.

This time period is also the time where you want to really hone in on your visual abilities. Make sure you are working on keeping the release point within the 6% of your center of focus. If the release point is in that 6%, you have a better chance of making the save. You must work on it. Now is the time to do it. Do not wait until the season starts to implement something so valuable.

Tryouts

In tryouts, it's very important to be in the right mind-set as soon as you walk onto the field. As you put on your equipment, imagine you are a gladiator getting ready for battle. It is crucial you take some time before practice to put yourself into a competitive state of mind.

Be sure to play to win during tryouts. The biggest mistake I see from goalies that need to improve their mental toughness is they play to impress. You must play to win. Which means stop the ball. Focus on the games or drill in front of you. Be loud! Bring it!

I see many goalies get so nervous during tryouts they cannot relax and play at the level they are accustomed to. That is because they are usually focusing on the result. Try to maintain focus on the process and not the result. In other words, stay in the present and do not try to forecast what could happen. Too many goalies let a couple in and then start to freeze because they think they just blew their chances. Fight the urge to feel that way. Stay focused on the next shot. The next shot is always more important than the last one.

Practice

During practice is your time to really hone your skills and build your talent. Once the season starts and you start playing and preparing for games, you will not get the ample time you need to improve your technique.

You must come to practice everyday ready to play. There are no days off when you want to be the best. You want to approach each day the same: Focused, intense, and always trying to improve. This is a critical point of practice.

Many goalies just go through the motions during practice. You must put energy into your practice and practice with intention. A goalie client once said, "but isn't practice in itself making me better?"

The answer is: Maybe. But only slightly. You must come to practice every day like it is a game. If you play at a high intensity level in a game, you must do the same in practice. Again, practice does not make perfect. Practice makes permanent. So, how you play in practice is how you will play in the game. Therefore how you prepare for games is how you should prepare for practice. Get it?

Game Day

Ok. So, this is it. This is what it all comes down to. Playing big in big games. So how do we do it?

It is most important that you realize that all the preparation for this moment started six months ago. You must lay the groundwork before this day, which means increasing confidence, working on tracking the ball from release to contact, knowing how intense you need to be to play your best, etc.

On game day, make sure you get enough sleep the night before. Remember, the studies tell us that sleep deprivation is a major component to slowing reaction times.

If you wake up anxious and stressed, go for a short jog early in the day. If the game is at 1:00, hit the road for a couple miles to drain some of that nervous energy.

Be sure to get to the locker room early. You do not want to be late for the pre-game meeting, as it will only increase your anxiety level. You want to use this time to go over the scouting report and get into a good confident state of mind. Music is a good idea for the hour or hours before a game. Light music to relax.

Heavy music to get fired up right before you go out. Try not to get too fired up too early before the game. It is mentally exhausting. This will all get easier with practice.

As you get dressed and start to get ready before heading out to the field, put on your equipment, as you are a gladiator getting ready for battle. I know it sounds corny, but it works, and no one will know what you're doing.

As you walk on the field, put your shoulders back and your chin up. This will give you a sense of confidence. Breathe in "dominance" and blow out "anxiety." This is your time. As you watch the other team warm up, think to yourself you own the other team. There is no shooter that can beat you. You are going to go all out today. It's your time. Get ready.

Start your warm-up slow but with intention. You must have high energy, but not too much in the beginning. Let it build as the warm-up goes on. Ask the other goalies to stand between the restraining line and the midfield line so that you can throw them outlet passes after each save.

Take your time between saves. This is not a race. Although the excitement of the game will cause you to move and think faster. Be sure to slow down. Breath. The game will be here soon enough. As you are warming up be sure to continue focusing on the ball at the release point all the way to the contact point.

Start building the "Bring It!" mindset. Let it overcome all your senses. You want them to shoot. It's your day. Come on…. Bring It!

As you stand there at midfield, waiting to shake the other goalie's hand, let your confidence envelop you. As you run back the goal for the start of the game, take a second to yourself and think about all the work you have done to get to this point. This is your time. You've earned this.

C'mon!!

BRING IT!!!

About the Author

C hris Buck has his Masters in Exercise and Sport Psychology and is a Certified Consultant and member of the Association for Applied Sport Psychology (AASP). He has consulted with professional and amateur athletes alike, implementing mental conditioning programs in a wide variety of sports, including lacrosse, golf, tennis, soccer, basketball, track/field, crew, fencing, hockey, and baseball.

Coach Buck works with multiple NCAA lacrosse programs as a Sport Psychology Consultant to the team as well as a Goalie Psychology Specialist. He is also the Goalie Psychology Specialist for G3 Lacrosse. He also wrote the Level 1, Level 2, and Level 3 goalie coaching certification materials for US Lacrosse.

He has worked with goalies all over the country and Canada who have committed to, or are playing at, elite programs such as Johns Hopkins, Syracuse, Drexel,

Ohio State, Notre Dame, Georgetown, Villanova, Rutgers, UVA, UPenn, Union, Tufts, etc. as well as working with several MLL professional goalies.

Coach Buck is the Assistant/Goalie Coach for the Northeast Team of the Underclassmen Under-Armour All-America Lacrosse Classic (2010 - Present). Chris is the Mental Coach and Goalie Specialist for the Avon Old Farms boy's varsity lacrosse team and was the Head Coach of the Desert Mountain High School women's lacrosse team, leading them to the 2008 Arizona state semi-finals. Additionally, he coached the Arizona State All-Star Team in the Women's National Tournament in Baltimore, MD ('08).

Chris grew up and played lacrosse in Wilton, CT, winning two state championships during his time there and finished his four-year high school career with a 46-1 record as the starting goalie. After high school, he played lacrosse at Ithaca College.

32182576R00082

Made in the USA
Middletown, DE
25 May 2016